SHAKING
THE
ETHER

IAIN CAMPBELL WEBB

PUBLISHED BY
LAPWING PUBLICATIONS
c/o DENNIS & RENE GREIG
1 BALLYSILLAN DRIVE
BELFAST BT14 8HQ

PRINTED BY

TEXTFLOW SERVICES
THE SCIENCE LIBRARY
LENNOXVALE
BELFAST

ISBN 1 898472 19 X
LAPWING POETRY PAMPHLET
Iain Webb: Shaking The Ether
PUBLISHED 1995
COPYRIGHT REMAINS WITH AUTHOR

Lapwing Publications gratefully acknowledge the financial assistance of the **Arts Council of Northern Ireland** and **The UK Foundation for Sport and the Arts** in the publication of this pamphlet.

CONTENTS

SOLILOQUY	7
SUGAR BABY	8
SHAKING THE ETHER	9
SYMPOSIUM	10
A HISTORY OF LOVE	12
SIBLING	14
INSTRUMENTAL	15
AIRFIXING	16
BLINKING	17
ALAUDIDAE	18
GRAN	23
SPEECHLESS	24
REPLICATION	25
CANARIES	26
TRAPIZIUM	27
TAXIDERMY	28
TONIGHT	29
BITTER SPRING	30
LEAVE TAKING	31

**DEDICATED TO THE MEMORY OF
MY DEAR MOTHER AND FATHER.**

*Stepping out now,
from long loving shadows
standing in your footprints
finding new roads
walking on my own feet.*

SOLILOQUY

Don't talk to me about the Queen
she's no time for me,
never gave me a second glance.
They said I was mad
to even try,
she was just too busy.
Banished from the royal court,
wandering through honeyed thoughts
tripping over this years children
as I went.
Philosophising on my place
in the hive-archy,
talking to myself again
asking the old question;
to bee, or not to bee.

SUGAR BABY

You cannot make a cake
without breaking eggs,
when my flour had fully risen
cooking steadily for nine months
peeping out cautiously
from the biological oven
reluctant to leave,
pushed out eventually
a steaming D.N.A. concoction.
Now my loving bakers have departed
taking years to appreciate
their rich list of ingredients.
They mix new constellations now
wonderful metaphysical
chocolate, marzipan, and coffee creations.
I sit on the kitchen table
buttered, jammed, and iced,
sprinkled by a hundred thousand
tiny inadequacies
loves, fears, ongoing education of the years.
Tasting sweet and sour dreams
never quite having your cake and eating it.
At long last
the final slice
melting on life's warm plate,
waits to be kissed
by heavenly lips.

SHAKING THE ETHER

The long sobs of Autumn violins
began playing fifty years ago.
My father a young musician
used his nimble fingers
on the hair trigger
necessities violently strung instruments,
part of a mighty orchestra
specialising in Beethoven's
three dots and a dash.
My father a young radio technician
along with a million others
courageously re-connected civilisation's wires,
relit hopes flickering flame
switched on the European lights.
Liberty's seed germinated
by precious life blood
struggles to bloom,
lift its tattered head
against tyranny's dark rain.
The long sobs of Autumn violins
still sounding
transmitting freedom,
wound my heart
with a monstrous languor.

SYMPOSIUM
(for Dennis & Rene Greig)

Finding myself at the world's end
in the company of poets
who silver tongued their way
through sun and rain.
Flowers write themselves wildly
telling of earthly love,
blooming typography
in a narrative style
geographically speaking!
How small the planet is tonight
this room lit by European wisdom
kindling fires.
Here if you shake a tree
a thousand words
come falling down,
pulling feathery parodies
from poets' mouths
to tickle cloudy ears.
Hearing angels laughing
they sing much older songs
out on a love's edge
soothing aged hearts.

Again myself finding
at the world's beginning
knee deep in similes
and smart metaphors,
cluttering up Sunday
when even God rested
I swept them all away,
leaving clever phrases
half-finished continents, animals,
and eight-legged men and women
before he thought of tarantulas
sticking in the bristles
like dog hairs
like the Donegal kindness perhaps:
newly created weather
takes a turn for the better
softly raining poems
waking the nimble big cats
that paw and claw and rip
at the fabric of thought.

A HISTORY OF LOVE

Last night you wandered out
about your girlhood
through those endless Summers
stepping over the sleeping rain
stifling yawns on river brown damask
losing itself in Neagh's easy going arms.
Secretly you entered O'Neill's domain
ancient woods welcomed children's laughter
days of perfect happiness
life in another green world.

Staying at her great uncle's cottage.
Next door when the picture-house closed
its last reel flickered to an end
neighbours collected rusting bicycles
that waited patiently in the yard,
he knew each foot fall
wished them all a goodnight.

Beside factory-sawtoothed roofs
continually cut out cloud designs
water dust clogged the teeth
blue flax sky spinning fine weather.
Everyone worked in an English owned mill,
village should have been renamed
from Randal's to Webbstown.

A little later touched by war's shadow
chance meetings outside
Belfast's central post office,
the west-country weaver
made his gossamer with care:
six months on entangled in a web of love,
she changed her name.

Children created at intervals
patchworked spiderlings
woven from Huguenot threads,
sowing parental tenderness into our anatomy.
While I try to catch thoughts
writing a history of love,
they have crossed the rubicon
conquering gravity,
spinning new star clusters.

SIBLING
(for Robert)

Growing under your four years shadow
fighting down the days,
caustic cutting look or word
escapes from eye or mouth,
passing the wrong hypercritical football
scoring own goals.
Walking carefully
among politically sensitive minefields
planted by uncle Joe,
brotherly disagreements melted
by laughter and tears,
same blood, skin, bones,
runs, drums, rattles,
plays a family music
time signatures beating sympathetically,
through him, through me.
Only yesterday noticed blotches
on backs of hands
our mother's and father's
epidermic embodiment.
We set off life sailing
charting genealogical progress,
in navigation around ourselves
exploring new found grandmotherly
islands.

INSTRUMENTAL

If instruments were buildings
for living in,
perhaps we could live
in finely constructed violins,
pluck their strings
enjoy the existence
inside their reverberating membranes,
experience
the creative interplay
between the instrument maker
and ourselves.
In the fine poetry
of imagination's architecture
it's difficult to keep
everything in tune.
If we continue pulling
each others' strings
eventually we will play well
together one day.
Harmony's subtle discovery
listening to humanity's
beautiful music.

AIRFIXING

He cycled every day into Belfast
through the weathered years
requisitioning modernity's engines
at the aircraft yard.
One Saturday we took the bus
childhood thoughts fuelled
by jet propulsion:
beyond hangar, being repaired,
a fighter stood impatiently
longing to sting cumulus again.
Imagined myself a pilot
sitting inside the Vampire's cockpit,
tripped a hundred switches
roaring loudly I took off
head in the clouds
to taste infinity.
Dad's outside
his face smiling then laughing
walking on a wing and a prayer.
At home we constructed airfix models
fusing fuselage, ailerons, and turboprops,
love, kindness, and understanding
built an aeroplane in a single afternoon
cementing father son relationship.
We used small tins of airforce grey
to paint the squadron
that flew in formation
from twisted cycle spokes
around the bedroom
my brother and I shared.
Engrossed in another daydream
wiping away a tear or two,
sitting on the bicycle bar
watched as he unfolded wings
took flight together:
over life over death flying into the sun.

BLINKING

The guardian angel's
flashing gemstone,
fitted snugly over his bony finger,
keeps his treasure close
holding himself in high regard.
Summer's fork-tailed fools
on clipped winds, waver
around multifarious green churches:
these plants draped on walls
ring their tiny blue bells.
Luminosity attracts flimsy moths
while ageless little Dracula's
swing into the beam
taking fluttering mouthfuls
before the light dissolves them.
Observed, slow dream-ships
wiggle down-lough
as meadow-sweet's smell
- nature's womanly guise -
fills my evening head.
Copeland's genuflection
sweeps across time
transcends universal space.
My Mother's spirit and I
walk the years
from white to black headlands
forever chasing shadows.
In the blink of an eye,
witnessed a single shooting star,
meteorites skimming between planets.
Lifetime
a swift brightness
against the dark.

ALAUDIDAE

1.

Spear of new land
head buried
in shifting granulation
forever halted flight,
never to complete arc
and incarcerate the Foyle,
thrusting into Inishowen's
green bleeding side.

Birds'-foot trefoil, delicately placed
setting dunes aflame
leaving sulphurous footprints.
Transported by a Saharan simoon
exotic visitors
two clouded yellows glowed
reappeared, not seen since 1936
survivors of the International Brigade.

2.

Rifles speak on a firing range
crackle and smack air,
shatter the peaceful moods
quarantined minutes.
Surprised a rusticated fox
gave a disregarding glance,
moved and induced ambiguity
between the bullets' heels.

Behind enemy lines
on a sabotage mission
Maoism's red and black heart,
eats the skylark's eggs
and breaks democracy's wings
outside the Forbidden City.
In all its 9,999 rooms
not a single bird sings.

3.

Alaudae arvensis launched itself
off the Martello Tower,
a streaked missile
upon changing forget-me-not sky.
Dazzled by allegro scherzando song
the spirits' revolutionary freedom,
Alouette des champs
expressing great virtuosity.

Exploded shells litter beach
shrapnel of Napoleonic wars,
land and sea's endless battlefield.
Cuirassiers' charging white horses
thunder down
smash the solid ranks,
infantries' rock-steady cliffs
in neo-classical time.

4.

At union of waters
sea drinks river.
Waders Winter station
followed magnetic migration lines,
feathered bio-engines
locomotion by star charts.

Skylark's singing
regains the marshalling yards
under Summers constellations.
Heavens watchmakers
keep their own aerial time,
gives an articulate voice
to the stratosphere.

5.

Ticking clouds
chime the quarter,
the half,
and the hour.
Near shore
enchanted by a wave-lullaby,
I fall asleep amid dunes
Lark's singing in my ear.

I had a joyous dream.
It was the year
the Generalissimo dies.
A calandra lark sang
high up,
over the Badalona promontory,
in Catalonia.
Song of the Republic.

6.

Wind-harp played an antiphon
on the plucked marram,
dune spider chased sand fleas
through my salt-washed hair,
beached mammal upon strand
lost wayward soul.
Slow rising sound
becoming song-storm.

No random jangled notes
motif of Da Da Da; Daaaa.
Lark's musical vocabulary
spans half the globe.
Reaches into nearly deaf ears,
opens closed abandoned hearts
across the space-time continuum.

7.

In the mountain meadows
he found himself
one transcendental Spring morning.
A ringdrossel
had followed his progress,
it sang to him weakly
stony voiced among stones
untutored imitation of the amsel.

Beautiful radiant song
cascaded from clouds,
a lark
orchestrated the landscape
Kappelmeister of the sky.
Ludwig wrote sketches in his notebook
smudged notation with a single tear.

8.

Taught pianoforte
by Albrechtsberger,
in the fields taking lessons
from Lullula Arborea,
a formidable songster.
Using slowed down recordings
someone wrote out its music,
discovered 230 notes every second.

Concept of reptilian brain
perhaps a common ancestry
crawling from primeval swamps..
One remarkable imagination
caught these sounds
used in compositions,
before the silence fell.
His great private grief.

9.

On hills above Belfast
lark sang its last evening arpeggio,
whispered sweet nothings
into Beethoven's ghostly ear.
Bonaparte swallowed another cloud country
for his supper,
closed his eyes and went to sleep.
Hummed themes from the Emperor Concerto
in dreams of triumph.

Having glorified music
and the skylark's celestial song,
5th Symphony of May passed
in Classical sonata form,
an exposition, development,
and recapitulation.
The sun made itself comfortable
he settled down to slumber
between mountain's motherly arms.

GRAN

At my Irish Argentinian Grandmother's house
two large pampas grass plants
grew in the garden
reminded her of the new world.
Taking tea was always an adventure
she reads the leaves
patterns of fortune or misfortune
trailed across china.
Shapes told stories,
a bird meant moving
a shoe going on a journey
a ship letters from afar
a broken heart love lost.
Told to be silent
when she took my Mother's sprained hand
closed eyes and spoke secret words
then I felt her charming magic.
Long gone now
passed over to the other side
she spends half the time
in South America,
chasing rheas
arm wrestling armadillos
horse back riding across flowering plains.
Visits Ireland often dodging reality
her gentle laughter
fell like showers of chuckles
She whispered a loving prayer
for all of us
between the wall clocks tocks,
sleeping soundly with dust
on the mantle piece of family memory.

SPEECHLESS

He never liked to talk about it
even as children we knew little,
I only remember brief snatches
it was all too horrible to think about
never mind putting images into words.
As a child having nightmares about one story,
how he picked up a German helmet
half a head in it
the brains hanging out.
Yet he was good at words,
writing letters home
for those who never wrote.
Carried a copy of Brooke's poems with him
in his kitbag throughout the second war,
emphasises his Englishness.
I imagined him reading a poem to my mother
sitting together below oak leaf shadow
dreaming of Wiltshire hills.
Stitched, his love for a northern girl
into rich tapestries
warming her shoulders
winning her kind strong heart.
He was far from speechless.

REPLICATION
(for Rachel)

Let's begin at a basic level, in conversational mode,
my Apple Mac maleness courting your I.B.M. femininity.
Maybe our programmes could interact, use binary notation
transactions between my C.P.U. and your C.P.U.
We might even be compatible.
Mathematical digits play upon your hard disc's heart
raising pulse beats a megacycle or so.
Just when I felt fully justified to attempt an interface,
you suddenly spoke FORTRAN, COBOL and even Pascal,
learning these languages quickly matching intelligence.
Knowing other peripheral units would find you attractive
worried in case mutual contact spread the virus,
- decided to keep my distance for awhile -
became polarised one from the other.
I tried, muttering away in alphanumeric computations
not being able to drive you from magnetic thoughts,
your powerful memory infiltrated my system
working an ambiguity-error, imprecise synchronisation.
Unexpectedly she re-opened communications,
clothed in completely new software
which old hardware found most appealing.
Her great grandfather was Babbage's Differential Machine.
She is third generation,
speaking quick megabytes, the critical path method
floating point representation. I am fourth generation,
a little smarter but none the wiser.
At last settling down in similar configurations
shared-resource and logic systems, undertake
    housekeeping routines.
Seeing through electronic disguises
joining in simultaneous input and output,
sparking together in real time processing
same electrical impulse birthing new generations of hybrids
I will be virtually yours, if you will be virtually mine.

CANARIES

In the shed he built himself
he kept canaries
that only sang when the sun shone.
How yellow they were
specks of solar flares,
fluttering.
One day the singing stopped,
red mite's army on manoeuvres
silenced melodious whistlings
murdered all his sopranos and baritones,
We buried bright bundles in the garden.
Starting from scratch
you acquired new stock,
family fondness for birds continued
brotherly love ran the hospital
for the lame and flightless.
Exchanging his terrestrial wings
my avian father's warbling
still echoes through
the feathered shadow of remembrance.

TRAPEZIUM

Inside sky blue domes, Gabrielle sat fishing for souls
espied a ravishing woman
swinging delightfully beneath a little canvas tent,
supple trapeze artist wearing cloud costumes
aroused unusual sensations under saintly garments
his wing feathers loosening strangely.
Slowly he felt less angelic
spent every minute by her side
somersaulting through space,
she quickly fell for him
he was always there, cushioning the descent.

Far above, the heavenly host muttered,
thinking it would not last.
Observing them naked together
falling silent,
how beautiful this human love was.
They enjoyed the high life together
walking emotional tightropes
no safety nets provided.
In the mornings she often wondered
where all this plumage came from.
When the boss whispered in his ear
that it could not be;
he had to return.

How typical it was
of this spirit, or ghost, or holy fool,
to leave her, like any other man.
A year later she mistimed a spin
during rehearsals, landing awkwardly.
That night performing in the Elysian circus
slipping peacefully into his eternal embrace
sleeping with angels.

TAXIDERMY

The street's electrodynamics
A powerful alternating under-current,
imprisoned secret water
seeks the Lough's freedom
having such a passionate anger
it tilts the great clock.

Indian-inked beetles
drew a line in the street,
glossy shell-cases open
rearrange wings before moving
their beating thorax
mechanical city's throbbing heart
wait to collect the nightly swarm.

On motorway the joyful hum
rhythmic rattle noticed at speed
put words to tarmacadamed music.
Conversation with driver -
bonus of front-seat occupation -
the stories he could tell.

Driving through rain sheaves
weather's cloud-handkerchief
wipes Napoleon's nose.
Vehicle tuts, shakes its head
philosophically,
longing for the old London routes.
Charing Cross, Cricklewood, Muswell Hill,
Hornsey Road, Trafalgar Square, Highgate.

TONIGHT

At this very tick of October
art nouveau vapour
twists round buildings,
enters Metro stations,
sits for awhile
spiralling on platforms.
Spirits walk chill boulevards
from Montparnasse and Pere Lachaise
recite stories of laughter and love
bending feminine Parisienne ears.
An open letter decorates floor
quickly read over croissant and coffee
now it conducts a dialogue with wood.
That evening in her creaky flat
she switched the light off,
a half-consumed baguette
cogitates its former wholeness,
sleeping table loses itself in woodlands
Curled up cat-like on easy chair
she purrs with pleasure home cottage dreaming.
Clothed in emerald velvet
blossoming of small breasts
softly fondled drumlins
sigh under sheep's' nibbling kisses.
Tonight my loneliness
caused shivers in the
Gutenberg discontinuity.
Plate tectonics of the heart
gradually
pulling me, pulling me,
asunder.
I plummeted off
the Richter scale
falling, falling,
saved by a lover's comforting grasp.

BITTER SPRING

At the hospital asking the way
walking forever to find her,
pink snow tumbled over shoes
blows along kerbstones,
above, delicate little parasols
unrolled from beech branches.

Spoke about the bush
we planted together,
it had produced
a single first bud.

How she loved her flowers,
distance grew gradually,
petals took longer to unfold,
sickness on an aged rose.
She died in the Summer
finally I emerged
to discover a bitter Spring,
looked through her eyes
across a vanished life.

I counted six magnolia blossoms
burning candles giving light
to this and other worlds.
She, re-grows everyday
touching her green fingers.

LEAVE TAKING

Assailed by a phone call
a voice said,
"please come straight away."
Becoming unhinged, panic sets in,
an automatic gesture
neighbour's car quickly commandeered -
heartlong rush to hospital.

In the small room she lay
struggling for life,
ship of breath's horrible gurgle
drowning under a cruel lung's sea.
Shaken, we three, her children
hold onto her for dear life.
Spoke words, spoke words.

In the small sigh of recognition
a leg movement the last sign,
shallow now, then shallower,
until the silent wave washed her shore.
A mother's powerful love
slipped soulfully beyond our reach,
hovered above us for awhile
before it stepped into the radiance.

I would not let her go
held her hand trying to warm it,
to bring her back, to bring her back.
My life blood
could not overcome coldness.
Room filled up with tears,
grief's pain-etched eyes,
death eats the heart.

Life passing,
a single wing beats.
Her being a small bird
trembling in my closed hands,
letting go is the hardest thing.
Time should be at a standstill
how could things go on.
I stumbled out
inhabiting a different planet.